I0816396

Words that are tricky to understand are in **bold**. Find out what they mean in the glossary.

Words that are difficult to say are in *italics*. Find out how to say them at the back of the book.

DO FISH ONLY LIVE UNDERWATER?

DISCOVER THE SCIENCE BEHIND **ICHTHYOLOGY**

(ICK-thee-OH-luh-jee)

Written by Olivia Watson
Illustrated by Valeria Abatzoglu

WHAT IS ICHTHYOLOGY?

Ichthyology is the scientific study of fish. It is a branch of **zoology.**

The scientists who study fish are called **ICHTHYOLOGISTS.**

Billions of years ago, our planet was completely covered in water. So it's not surprising that scientists think fish were some of the **first animals on Earth!**

But they didn't look much like the fish we see today. Earth has changed a lot over time – fish have had to change too to survive in their changing **environments.**

That's where *ichthyologists* come in! These scientists don't just identify **species** of fish – they look at where fish live, how they interact with plants and other animals, and how they **adapt** to different **habitats**. This helps them understand fish, as well as our natural world as a whole. Ichthyologists know fish are incredible at adapting to their environments, but could they really live anywhere?

Wherever they live, fish have to find ways to avoid being eaten by **predators**! Today, millions of fish live in shallow coral reefs where there's a high risk of being eaten! One way fish stay safe is by making themselves hard to find. Tiny clownfish have a special body coating which lets them hide safely inside anemones **that sting other fish!**

While many species like shallow waters, some fish prefer greater depths – even parts of the ocean that are so deep light never reaches them!

These are tricky waters to survive in, so it can be hard to find food this deep. But that's not a problem for female anglerfish, which have their own headlamps! They grow a light that hangs off their forehead to attract **prey**, allowing them to thrive in pitch-black waters.

It’s cold in the oceans’ depths, but the coldest waters of all are found at the North and South poles. In these places, where it seems nothing could survive, scientists made an incredible discovery.

Several fish, including Antarctic icefish, create special **proteins** to stop their blood from freezing. This means they can survive in temperatures that would normally **freeze a body solid!**

Fish also need special skills to live where it's very hot. Higher temperatures are difficult for many fish to deal with as there is less **oxygen** in warm water. Like us, fish need oxygen to live. The difference is they breathe by taking it from water, using their **gills**.

Desert pupfish survive in their hot home by holding their breath for **five hours at a time!**

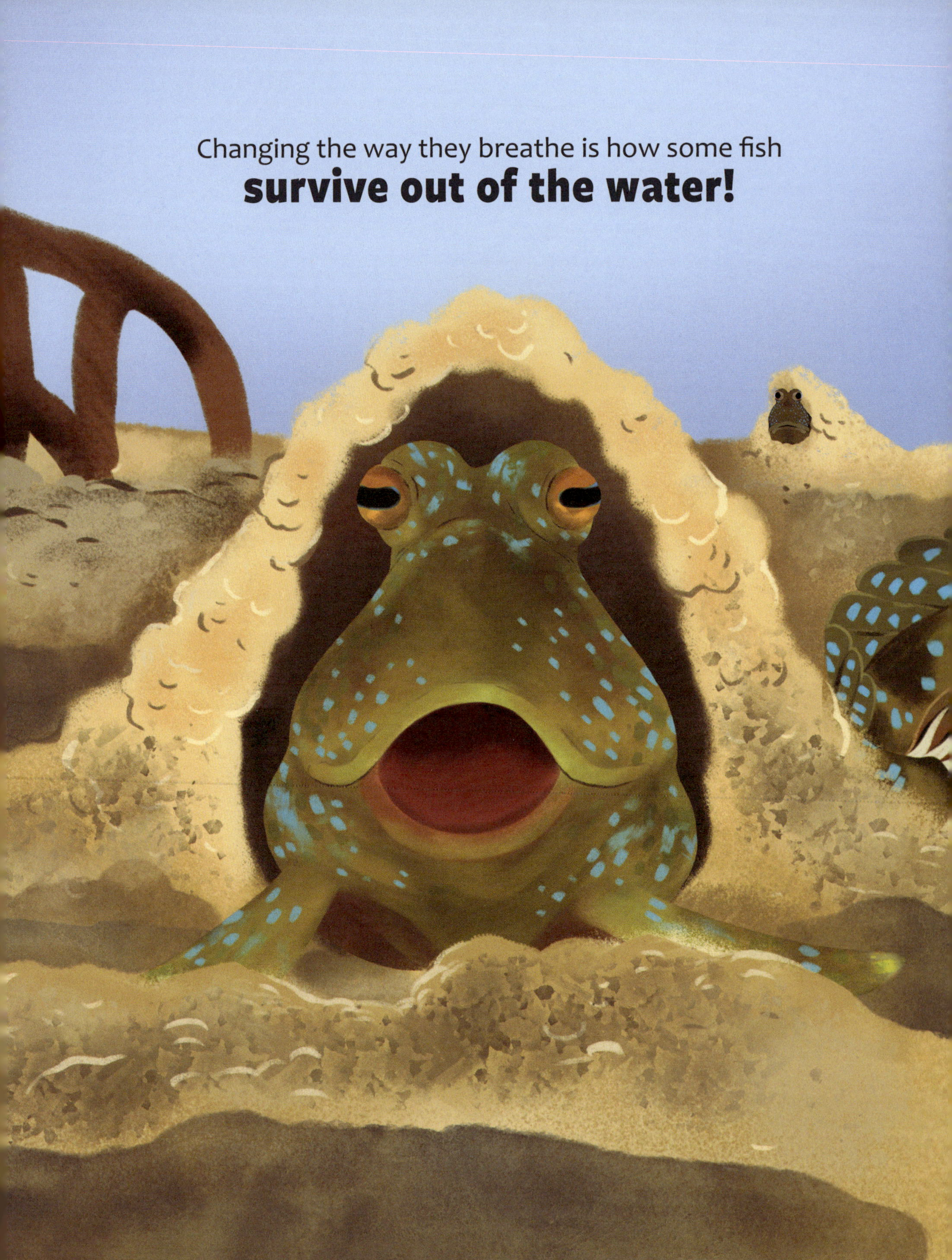
Changing the way they breathe is how some fish
survive out of the water!

Mudskippers hold bubbles of water in their gills so they can keep breathing while on land. They can also **absorb** oxygen through their skin! These abilities help these swamp-dwellers stay near their muddy burrows, where their eggs are hidden, even when the water has gone out.

African lungfish also use similar abilities as rivers in their floodplain homes often dry up. But they have adapted one step further. As well as gills for breathing underwater, these fish have true **lungs** for breathing air through their mouth or nose!

In dry seasons, they burrow underground, leaving a small gap for air and enter a state of **hibernation** until water comes back. They can survive there for up to five years!

The walking catfish can also survive out of water, but only if its skin stays moist! It mostly travels between nearby places of **freshwater** in search of a **mate**, food, or to escape from becoming a predator's food!

This clever fish uses its front fins to stay upright as it wriggles across the land, a bit like a snake slithering.

It's not just walking catfish that do this! Other species, like snakeheads, also travel over land when their environment is no longer suitable or safe to live in. By tracking fish, scientists can learn what's happening in nature, like if the **food chain** has changed, the water has become too dirty, or the **climate** has got warmer.

Fish don't just tell us about the natural world, they do a lot to help it too! Whether on land or water, fish poop contains lots of **nutrients**, which plants need to grow and stay healthy…

fish keep the food chain balanced – as predators, they stop the number of animals, like insects and shrimp, from getting too high, and as prey, they are the food for larger animals...

and others even help different animals. Some brave fish attach themselves to whales! The fish eat the **parasites** living on them, which keeps whales healthy while the fish get an easy meal in return.

Fish are great at adapting, but it takes thousands of years. If environments change too quickly and fish can't keep up, they face **extinction**. That's why ichthyologists' work is so important – they know when fish are in danger and need help.

Fish are an important food for humans and move nutrients around the planet's waters to keep them healthy, so saving fish is essential!

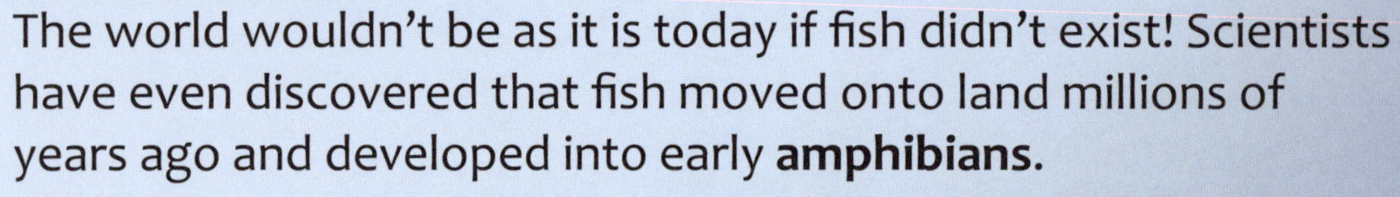

The world wouldn't be as it is today if fish didn't exist! Scientists have even discovered that fish moved onto land millions of years ago and developed into early **amphibians.**

While there are more than 100 species of fish living today that can survive on land, this ancient discovery teaches ichthyologists this is something fish have been able to do for years and years!

Fish

LIVING ON LAND

Scientists have discovered lots of different species of fish that can survive on land. Here's just a few amazing facts about them!

EPAULETTE SHARK

The *epaulette* shark is also known as the "walking shark". This animal uses its fins to crawl between rock pools when on the hunt for prey at low tide.

MUDSKIPPER

Mudskippers get their name from their habit of skipping across the mud in their swampy homes. They are so well-adapted that they find it easier to hunt on land than in water!

CLIMBING PERCH

This small freshwater fish can survive out of water as long as its skin stays moist. It travels across land in search of food or a healthier habitat.

AFRICAN LUNGFISH

This impressive fish is one of the longest surviving animal species on Earth. Scientists think it has been around for nearly 400 million years!

SENEGAL BICHIR

Similar to the African lungfish, the *Senegal bichir* has both gills and lungs, so it can live in water or on land, depending on the weather conditions in its habitat.

Fantastic

FISH FACTS

There's so much to discover about the world of ichthyology. Do you know the answers to some of the world's biggest questions about fish?

HOW MANY FISH SPECIES ARE THERE?

Scientists have discovered more than 32,000 species of fish. Amazingly, they find hundreds of new species every year, so the total number of fish species is always changing!

ARE SHARKS FISH?

Yes! All sharks are fish. In fact, the biggest fish in the world is the whale shark, which can grow to be as long as a bus!

WHAT'S THE OLDEST FISH SPECIES?

The *coelacanth* is one of the oldest living species. Scientists thought it became extinct with the dinosaurs millions of years ago. Then it was caught by a fisherman in 1938!

DO FISH SLEEP?

Yes! But most fish don't have moveable eyelids. Instead, they have a see-through layer protecting their eyes. So even when they're asleep it looks like their eyes are open! The only fish with closing eyelids are sharks.

HOW DO FISH COMMUNICATE WITH EACH OTHER?

Different types of fish communicate in different ways. Many, including parrotfish, use sounds like clicking, honking, and grunting to send messages to each other. Others use smell, movements, or electrical signals.

GLOSSARY

Absorb – to take in.

Adapt – when a living thing develops special features or skills to help it survive in its environment.

Amphibians – cold-blooded animals that live both in water and on land. Examples include frogs and toads.

Climate – long-term temperatures and weather conditions.

Environments – everything that is around us.

Extinction – when a plant or animal species no longer exists.

Food chain – the order in which different animals eat each other to survive.

Freshwater – water that is naturally not salty.

Gills – the body part that lets fish breathe underwater.

Habitats – the places where animals and plants live.

Hibernation – a deep sleep-like state that can last for weeks, months, or years.

Lungs – the body part that lets animals and humans breathe air.

Mate – one of a pair of animals that live or have babies together.

Nutrients – substances or ingredients that plants and animals need to live and grow.

Oxygen – an invisible gas that plants produce, and people and animals need to breathe.

Parasites – living things that live on or in another living thing, often causing harm.

Predators – animals that hunt other animals for food.

Prey – an animal that is hunted by other animals for food.

Proteins – tiny building blocks that help our bodies grow and stay strong.

Species – a group of living things that share characteristics and features, and produce young together. For example, goldfish and clownfish are different species.

Zoology – the scientific study of animals. *Need help saying this? Look below!*

HOW DO I SAY?

Coelacanth
SEE-luh-kanth

Epaulette
eh-puh-let

Ichthyologist
ICK-thee-OH-luh-jists

Ichthyology
ICK-thee-OH-luh-jee

Senegal bichir
seh-nuh-gawl bee-shur

Zoology
zoo-OH-luh-jee

THE BIG QUESTIONS ANSWERED

This is more than just a series of books; it is a complete resource. Accompanying each book is a variety of FREE material to engage curious kids with science.

www.thebigquestionsanswered.com

Use the QR code to visit the website, download free resources, and discover other books in the series.

On the website, find out incredible things about ichthyologists, including what they do, some of their greatest discoveries, and the people who have made a difference in this field of science.

The material is also available for home or classroom use, supporting all the information in this book.

Teachers' & Parents' Resources
With discussion prompts and questions, extra information, and facts around key topics.

Young Ichthyologists' Activity Pack
Fun activities for wannabe fish experts, including creative writing, drawing, word searches, and much, much more.

The Big Questions Answered is published by Beetle Books. Beetle Books is an imprint of Hungry Tomato Ltd.

First published in 2025 by Hungry Tomato Ltd
F15, Old Bakery Studios, Blewetts Wharf, Malpas Road, Truro, Cornwall, TR1 1QH, UK.

ISBN 9781835691465

A CIP catalog record for this book is available from the British Library.

With thanks to:
Editors: Holly Thornton and Millie Burdett
Designers: Amy Harvey and Meg Holbrook
The team at Beehive Illustration
Consultant: Tom Horton

Information in this book is up to date as of the time of writing.

Printed and bound in China.

Picture Credits:
(t = top, b = bottom, m = middle, l = left, r = right)
Shutterstock: AlessandroZocc 35tl; ArliftAtoz2205 33mr; Chanakan_Gallery 33br; Jalvan 35mr; jindrich_pavelka 32ml; Krzysztof Odziomek 34bl; Lovely Bird 33tl; Rich Carey 32br; silvae 34mr; Tatiana Belova 35bl.